HORATIO PARKER

AMS PRESS
NEW YORK

DELIVERED BEFORE THE
AMERICAN ACADEMY OF ARTS AND LETTERS
XXV JULY MCMXX

1863.1920

HORATIO PARKER

BY

GEORGE W. CHADWICK

NEW HAVEN

YALE UNIVERSITY PRESS

1921

Library of Congress Cataloging in Publication Data

Chadwick, George Whitefield, 1854-1931.
 Horatio Parker.

 Reprint of the 1921 ed.
 1. Parker, Horatio William, 1863-1919.
ML410.P163C4 1972   780'.92'4 [B]   72-1392
ISBN 0-404-08304-8

ML
410
.P163
C4
1972

Reprinted from the edition of 1921, New Haven
First AMS edition published in 1972
Manufactured in the United States of America

International Standard Book Number: 0-404-08304-8

AMS PRESS INC.
NEW YORK, N.Y. 10003

HORATIO PARKER

HORATIO PARKER, composer, conductor, organist and teacher, inherited from both parents an uncommonly retentive and alert mind and an artistic temperament; from his mother, also musical talent, or at least musical taste. His father was a well-known architect. Several large edifices in Boston and other cities of New England are specimens of his work. He was for some time superintendent of construction of the Boston Post Office and other public buildings in Massachusetts, and was a man of wide and varied knowledge.

Parker's mother, daughter of a Baptist minister, was a woman of great refinement

5

and cultivation. An excellent Latin and Greek scholar, she had also considerable facility as a writer of English verse. To the care of four children she added the duties of organist in the village church at Auburndale and gave music lessons besides.

Undoubtedly Parker owed to her, who was his first teacher, the love of good music which became the passion of his life. As a boy he gave little indication of this. The woods of Auburndale and the Charles River (near which he lived) occupied much more of his attention than his piano practice. At fourteen he could hardly play a simple scale on the piano, but shortly after that his soul awakened to the beauty of music, especially of harmony, for which his latent talent developed with great rapidity. At sixteen he became organist of a small Episcopal church in Dedham, Massachusetts, and at once began to compose hymn tunes, anthems, and services for the choir. For the next two years he had lessons in pianoforte and harmony with various Boston teachers and made great progress.

At eighteen his ambition reached out toward orchestral composition. In this he was probably stimulated by the recent success of John K. Paine's two symphonies and of other American composers. It was at this time that my acquaintance with him began. He had already acquired remarkable facility in harmony and modulation, to which was added a very fertile vein of lyric melody, and both his melodies and harmonies had a distinct and individual character of their own, which may be detected in his later and more mature compositions. It was easy to predict even then that this combination of qualities would carry him far.

As my pupil he was far from docile. In fact, he was impatient of the restrictions of musical form and rather rebellious of the discipline of counterpoint and fugues. But he was very industrious and did his work faithfully and well. His lessons usually ended with his swallowing his medicine, but with many a wry grimace. It was quite natural that before long our relation should develop from that of teacher and pupil into a warm and sincere friendship, as it ever afterward remained.

It was during this period that he wrote the beautiful "Twenty-third Psalm" for women's voices and organ, revised and published some years after with harp and violin obbligato. In 1882, he went to Munich and entered the Royal Music School, in Rheinberger's class both in organ playing and in composition.

8

Rheinberger, although a composer of operas, orchestral works and of much romantic and beautiful chamber and choral music, was, as a teacher, conservative, almost to the verge of pedantry. Under his rigorous discipline Parker acquired that mastery of contrapuntal choral writing which so distinguished his later work.

While in school he wrote several works for orchestra and chamber music which were performed at school concerts. At his graduation in 1885 a cantata for chorus, solos, and orchestra, called "King Trojan," was performed under his own direction. Although this work showed some of the naïve qualities of youth and inexperience, its spirit was so fresh and spontaneous, and its construction and instrumentation so sure and authoritative, that it must be considered a remarkable effort for a young student of twenty-two. It was afterward performed at the Worcester Festival and in several other places.

He returned to America in 1885 and for the next seven years lived in New York. He took charge of the music department of the Cathedral School at Garden City and was afterward appointed as instructor at the National Conservatory, at the same time fulfilling his duties as organist at St. Andrews Church and later at Holy Trinity. Much of his church and organ music dates from this period, although he also wrote some secular choral works and piano music.

In 1891, during a period of serious ill health and of poignant domestic grief, he began the composition of "Hora Novissima." He had made a beginning on another mediæval Latin hymn, "Vita nostra plena bellis," but abandoned it on account of the monotony and inflexibility of the rhythm. The great hymn of Bernard, which is the foundation of several of our best-loved modern hymns of the church, was in the same collection of poetry. Probably encouraged by his mother, who made the translation for him, he set to work on the "Hora Novissima." It was finished in 1892 and sent in for the prize offered by the National Conservatory for a work for chorus and orchestra. It did not receive the prize, which was awarded to him for a much less important though charming work called "The Dream King and His Love."

"Hora Novissima" was performed for the first time by the Church Choral Society of New York on May 2, 1892, at the Church of Zion and St. Timothy, under his own direction. It was immediately recognized as an important work of permanent value. Performances in Boston by the Handel and Haydn Society in February, 1894, and at the Springfield Festival of the same year were succeeded by many others in different cities of the country, and eventually in England, where it has been performed more than twenty times. The solid musical worth of "Hora Novissima," its skillful and impressive choral writing, the poetic beauty of the solos, and the varied and colorful instrumentation, endear it to musicians, while its lofty spiritual atmosphere, its fervent religious expression, although tinged with a romantic mysticism, make a strong appeal to the general musical public.

In 1898 Parker was called to Boston to assume the position of organist and choirmaster at Trinity Church. The close proximity of his old home, the congenial companionship of his old friends, the active musical life of Boston, his growing reputation, all stimulated him to further effort. In

December, 1893, he wrote his ballad for baritone and orchestra, "Cahal Mor of the Wine-red Hand." This strange and remarkable poem by James Clarence Mangan made a strong appeal to his imagination and he produced a score that in dramatic power, poetic suggestion and vivid orchestral coloring has seldom been surpassed in this form by any American composer.

When, in 1894, the department of music at Yale University was reorganized as a completely equipped school of theoretical and applied music, he was appointed as its head, receiving at the same time the honorary degree of M. A. He was at first rather reluctant to accept this position, involving as it did the necessity of lecturing on Musical History and Æsthetics, of which he had never made any special study. But this deficiency was very soon made up, and his general lectures soon became an important as well as popular part of the curriculum. He organized and conducted a symphony orchestra, which became an indispensable laboratory of the department, since it furnished the necessary experience for composers, conductors, singers, and players who were studying in the school. During his administration the great organ in Woolsey Hall was built, to be succeeded after some years by a still mightier instrument. He also lived to see his department housed in a beautiful and fully equipped building of its own through the munificence of Mrs. F. S. Coolidge, herself a cultivated musician and the daughter of a Yale graduate.

Of Professor Parker as a teacher, others may speak with more authority than I. From his comprehensive knowledge of the classics as well as his sympathy with modern developments, his profound knowledge of, and masterly command of counterpoint and form, his genius for tone-painting with the orchestra, strikingly demonstrated in his operas, he was eminently fitted to be a guide and leader of young composers. He gave them his unstinted interest in the classroom and out, and some of them have risen to very honorable positions. He was succeeded by one of them as Dean of the Music School at Yale, and many there are to call him blessed.

In 1897 he wrote his oratorio of "St. Christopher." The poem of this work was written by his mother and was a labor of love. Working side by side, the poem and music grew at the same time. He introduced into this work two Latin hymns, one of which, "Jam sol recedit," is an unsurpassed masterpiece of choral writing for unaccompanied voices. "St. Christopher" was first performed by the Oratorio Society of New York under

Walter Damrosch in 1898, shortly afterward at the Springfield Festival, and in 1902 at both the Norwich and Bristol Festivals in England. It has never achieved the great popularity of "Hora Novissima" but is still in the repertoire of choral societies.

In 1899 he was invited to England to conduct "Hora Novissima" at the Three Choir Festival at Worcester. Both he and his work were welcomed with such enthusiasm that he was invited to contribute a new work to the Hereford Festival of the next year. Here the Wanderer's Psalm (the 107th, called the "Cantus Peregrinus") was produced. In the same year "Hora Novissima" was performed at Chester. This was followed by the "Star Song," a poem by Henry Bernard Carpenter, for the Norwich Festival in 1902 (for this piece he had already received the Paderewski prize), and "St. Christopher" at Bristol.

The same year he received the degree of Mus. Doc. from Cambridge University. If we consider the conservatism of English musical taste, especially in Cathedral towns, we must admit that this is rather a remarkable record for a young American in his thirties. The prophet is not without honor in England, at any rate.

For the Bicentennial of Yale University in 1902 he composed a Greek ode for male chorus and orchestra—the "Hymnos Andron"—a piece of singular power and beauty. He returned from England in order to conduct it at the Bicentennial exercises.

In 1911 he won the prize offered by the Metropolitan Opera Company for the best grand opera written in English and composed by an American, which was his opera "Mona," the libretto by Brian Hooker. In 1914 he won a similar prize offered by the Women's

Federated Musical Clubs with his opera "Fairyland," the libretto by the same poet.

This is not the proper time or occasion for a critical estimate of his two operas. He had little sympathy for the conventions and the artificialities of the stage, and perhaps he was lacking in what the Germans call *theatre blut*. This, combined with inexperience in composing for the stage and plots which made little appeal to the average theatre-goer, militated against the popular success of these works, but they proved his complete mastery of modern harmony and modern orchestration, and both of them were awarded valuable prizes. In the case of "Mona" it was the unanimous opinion of the judges that no other award was possible.

In his morality play, "The Dream of Mary," which he wrote in collaboration with John Jay Chapman, he returned to simple form of expression appropriate to such an art form. The characters narrate the story as well as sing; the audience takes part as in the Greek chorus, assisted by the choral forces on the stage. The atmosphere of the work is profoundly devout and religious.

Another work in which he collaborated with Mr. Chapman is a masque or serenata called "Cupid and Psyche"—a delightful composition in which, with very simple means, he has reflected the spirit of the Italian Renaissance. It was performed at Yale University in 1915.

In his last work, the music to the commemorative poem by Brian Hooker, in memory of the Yale men who gave their lives to their country in the late war, Parker has written his own Requiem. To this noble poem he has given a very impressive setting, elegiac in spirit but with some thrilling dramatic touches, as for instance at the words "One shall have sweet sleep"—the trumpet is heard in the distance sounding taps. It is an heroic tribute to heroic men, some of whom were his own students.

After he went to Yale he developed a decided literary ability. To a close and discriminating observation he added an individuality of expression, illuminated by gleams of pungent humor which caused him to be sought after as a speaker and contributor to various periodicals. His essay on contemporary music, delivered before the American Academy of Arts and Letters, is a good example of his ability in this direction. The individuality of his style was no less evident in his literary work than in his music.

He was fond of making paradoxical observation, sometimes rather difficult for less subtle minds to follow. Of a certain piece for organ and orchestra he said, "That has no business to sound so well." This was really a retroverted compliment to the composer for making a successful mixture of organ and orchestral tone, a problem which requires an expert musical chemist. Berlioz said that the orchestra was king and the organ was pope, and when they came together there was usually a clash.

As a musician, Parker's instrument was the organ. His master, Rheinberger, admired his playing and delegated him to play the solo part at the first performance of his concerto in F major. He continued his duties as organist at Trinity Church in Boston for six years after he went to New Haven, making the journey each week for the purpose. While making no pretensions as an organ virtuoso he often gave recitals, and in 1903 performed his organ concerto, then new, with the Chicago Symphony Orchestra, and shortly afterwards with the Boston Symphony Orchestra in Boston. This work, noble and dignified in character, is an important addition to the rather meagre repertory of compositions for organ and orchestra. He held an organ position in New York until a few years before his death, and conducted two singing societies in Philadelphia at the same time.

With his masterly command of orchestral resources it seems strange that he should have composed so little for the orchestra alone. He was often urged to do so and he would not have lacked a hearing. The symphony orchestras of America and probably of England were open to him, but he felt that he needed words as a vehicle and poetry for his inspiration, and in writing for voices he was in his element. His most important composition for orchestra alone is the "Northern Ballad," first performed by the Boston Symphony Orchestra, and afterwards in Chicago and other places.

He wrote with great facility, and his industry was prodigious. With all his varied activities as teacher, conductor, and organist, he kept steadily at composition, and in the summertime he allowed nothing—even his favorite golf or his bicycle—to interfere with it.

As a congenial companion, a loyal comrade, and a steadfast friend, Parker has left a blessed memory. His conversation, punctuated with keen wit, was stimulating, and not of the prima donna variety. Devoted as he was to his own art, he found time to be interested in politics, in literature, and in other arts. His mind was stored with a variety of information, and his memory was as remarkable for facts as it was for music.

His judgment was sound, and based on a comprehensive knowledge of the musical art. While his musical creed was founded on beauty of design, melodic breadth, and logical structure, he was interested in all modern developments in harmony and instrumentation. He had a singularly open mind in regard to modern compositions, and often expressed himself enthusiastically about some of the most "advanced" of them. Often he would say, "That is not as bad as it sounds." But with pretence or shams of any kind he had no patience, and he was quick to detect them in some of the modern fads of polyharmony and polycacophony.

He was fond of outdoor life, and an ardent devotee of golf and the bicycle. Many of his summers were spent in the vicinity of Tegernsee in the Tyrol, where he tramped in the mountains and rode his bicycle as a relaxation from his work. His amiability and cheerfulness never forsook him, even during the painful attacks of rheumatism from which he suffered all his life.

With the remarkable success of "Hora Novissima" both in America and in England, it was natural that his anthems, services, and hymns for the church should have achieved great popularity. He was easily the most distinguished musician in the American church, and it was perhaps inevitable that he should be classed as an ecclesiastic composer. But he was not a mystic or an ascetic; he was a simple, devout Christian gentleman who loved his church and all her offices, and he gave the best that was in him to her service. In the very last year of his life he gave valuable assistance to the commission on the revision of the hymnal.

But many pages of his music, from "Cahal

Mor'' throughout his orchestral works and operas, show that his real place is among the romanticists, and it is a high one. He was an honor to the name of American musician, and he commanded respect for it not only in his own country, but abroad.